Basic Genealogy

By Shannon Lefebvre

First Edition, 2017

Basic genealogy

So, you would like to learn more about your family? This is an absolutely fascinating pursuit, as the stories emerge and people talk and you find new documents. If you are going to start your family tree, then you will need to find the following for each person if possible. Each area will include a rough breakdown and some hopefully humorous tips to help.

Birth date

Birth date is more than just their birthday, but also the location of the birth if known. If you have a commoner type of name such as Mary Smith, this may be critical in distinguishing your grandmother from the other Mary Smiths. Also, please list any unusual circumstances. Unusual circumstances can include being born surrogate, the sole survivor with still born siblings, or of a multiple birth (twins, triplets, etc.), and are often denoted as (twin) behind the name.

Death Date

Death comes to us all eventually. If possible, find the death certificate or military records, depending on the death circumstances. Cause is also important. Most people will end up dying of a known problem, such as heart disease. A few have death records with ongoing inquests, and that requires more following up. It is also unfortunately common in past eras to change the cause of death to hide deaths caused by venereal illness, alcohol or drugs, or the plague. The last chunk of this information block includes burial information. Are they in a public or private cemetery? Do they have a headstone? Have they been moved? Or were their ashes sprinkled at the beach?

Emigration/Immigration and Naturalization records

Emigration and immigration both refer to the relocation of a family or individual, whether that is to a new town or to a new country. In the modern world, families rarely stay in one place for generations anymore, and so this is critical. Many records are now digital, including Ellis Island and other sites, and classically historians have listed emigrants by categories in written reference books available at special interest libraries. Try to locate the names of the ports and ships that are involved, who they travelled with, etc. Naturalization refers to the changing of one's legal national status. If you move to a new country, you can remain a resident alien (legal term) or you can choose to naturalize, which can give you more rights such as voting. There is also dual citizenship in certain cases, when individuals choose to be citizens of two countries at once.

Marriage records

Marriage records can include marriage certificates, announcements of engagements, etc. Marriage records' definition can also be stretched to include cohabitation of socially accepted pairs of adults who form families in their own way, or even religious orders marrying the nuns to God. These records also need to include if possible a location, which can give clues to residency and faith, and full correct names of all involved. This also includes the less happy side of divorce. Let's be honest, in a perfect world, marriage would last forever. But in the case of divorce, when did it occur? Who got custody? Or, alternatively, did they throw a Divorce party for the newly single folks?

Education history

It is only relatively recently that schooling has become mandatory to a point in the Western World. It remains a question even on job applications as to your highest complete grade level in 2017. In previous eras, many people worked without going to school first. Many otherwise very intelligent people could even argue in court and elsewhere without the benefit of being literate. Colonial iron industry magnates, in selected example, were schooled for a while and then apprenticed and did well for themselves. So, if you know that your family member has a PhD, write it down. If you know that they went to school through eighth grade, that is okay. Write it down.

Any formal titles and the reason for the title

Germany had abolished formal social titles such as Count and Baron after World War I, but the families are still around. If your family has a claim to an inherited title, understand the route that claim takes via inheritance and legality. Watch for last names that tell you about the background: LeRoy is "of the King"- why? LeComte- "Of the Count." See reference sources of your choice for your specific culture as to how to recognize illegitimate children of royalty, etc. William the Conqueror was a King, but did not have formal title beyond Duke originally, despite being recognized as royal on his father's side. There are also famous family names that are traceable.

Medical History

There should ideally be no stigma in illness, but it does change the course of a life sometimes. Helen Keller was blind and deaf. Famous physicists can be paralyzed but able to work. Some children and adults are unfortunately handicapped by mental or physical illness such that they may not live as full a life as others, or may adapt their skills to new pursuits. Military veterans and those in hazardous settings may have injuries resulting from circumstances. Sometimes you just need to know if they have spina bifida, asthma (for health history reasons of descendants), or a limp because they got hurt by a horse or falling back down a ventilation shaft during a prison break.

Military history

Military history can include any side of any war, any rank or office. Try to find any medals earned, and how they were recruited and discharged. List the branch and ranks they held, which wars and side of the war, their training, and dates of service. Some folks are known to have survived Andersonville, for example, or to have been shot for punishment by the military, and this tells you quite a bit. They may qualify for full military burial or choose to be more civilian. Markers at the cemetery, metal or flags, commonly denote this information in brief form. In case of major war, burial may be inexact, depending on the outcome of a battle and the ability to get the bodies home for family ceremonies.

Legal history

This category can be a bit touchy. Nobody wants to be known as a chicken thief all their life, or to have lost their license five times for DUIs, much less as a bigamist or other social act. Yet, that is part of their life and history. It can change the course of their families' lives via custody changes, divorce, etc. Hopefully the black sheep gets a bath, but if they do not they are no less human and should be recorded. The US and Australia have many of interesting early history, as the British government used them to send over not only impoverished indentured servants (often younger siblings who did not have a place on the farm or business at home), ex-privateers or possibly pirates, and other prison-crowded help that were thieves or other categories, to work out their sentences in the new territories. Many died in the new environments, but many also loved and married and grew old. Sometimes life offers you hard choices to survive.

Work history

Work history consists of what type of work the person performed, where, and when. Look at the last name and find a good reference source. Many last names give you an original profession held by a family member: Carpenter, Taylor, Carter, Hunter, as examples. But individuals who inherit the name must be traced individually. It can help to find that so and so worked in a floral shop when he was younger. If there are only three floral shops in the right town at that time, you can narrow the field. If they have a common name, it can help get the right person for your tree. One example from Chester County, PA has one person working as a laborer most of their life, but during the Revolutionary War he carted ammunition down to General Greene from Pennsylvania to North Carolina, at the hazard of his life as his landlord was under British arrest for noncooperation.

Significant hobbies and interests

There is more to life than work. What hobbies did the person have? Were they part of a motorcycle group, racing horses, gardening, coaching a Scout troop, quilting, or a musician in the local band? Did they collect, write, read, lecture, raise seeing eye dogs, or volunteer at the homeless shelter? Did they teach or preach at church, bike around the world just to do so, or rebuild old cars?

Addresses for home

This category seems like a basic set of information used for clearances- and it is for living folks. But you need to know when the person moved to a new area if possible. In an increasingly mobile world, you can live and die anywhere in the world. In older trees, you may be called by where you live at the time, or which business you run if you buy it from someone else. The author has found twenty-seven people with her exact first and last name on Facebook. You must know who they are as distinct sets of choices to tell which one is right. In the Potts family tree (held on ancestry for viewing), there are nine David Pottses at once in the 18th century. They had to be distinguished, so Mrs. James tells us, by "Pine Forge David", etc.

Parents' names

It is a basic safety function to teach small children their correct name and those of their family members, so if, Heaven help us, there is a kidnapping, they know who they are. This also goes for genealogy. You need to know the parents' proper names, even if they elect to use a middle name because their first name is something like Horatio and they were teased in school. Other critical bits include any adoption information, including birth parents' and adoptive parents', and female maiden names. In a diverse world, some ladies change their names. Due to circumstances, guys can also change their names at marriage. Historically, it may have been done to preserve a family name which had only a daughter. Today, it is sometimes done to help with repeated family names in confused records. Stepfamilies are also family. They may be the only family a child knew. So, work in the step-family side as well.

Siblings' names

Siblings can help identify a commonly-named individual or they can serve as a search network.

Some families are huge. Others, depending on circumstances, end up as a single or no children, or may include adopted children (formal or informal) or grandchildren as children. By tracing sibling names, you may be able to learn more about an individual from letters, obituaries, or the newspapers.

Spouses' names

Yes, I hear you talking to the book- I know, I know, the spouses are important. But it can be a challenge when you have a large family you are looking for and the spouse is labelled "Mother". What was her birth name? Was she married before that marriage you sprang from? Unusual names can make tracing someone easier. Marriages that did not take well or ended may result in forgetting they existed for the sake of social acceptance, and to a loss of information.

Children's names and birth years

The children's' names are also critical. Recall that in past eras we did not have the same level of medical care available, and child mortality was higher. In a newer obituary, they may list the grown children with their married names. (See in-laws below). In older families, they may have four children when the parents die, but have delivered twelve infants to get those four to adulthood. There are also circumstances where a name is used for one child and they die young, and another child is given the name to save the memory. Or, for religious reasons, they may have the same baptismal name in front. They are still individual people.

In-law's names

Most wedding announcements and obituaries include the statutory information about the parents of the couple. This is critical information. These can mean major social linkages on either a local scale or (to use a recent tabloid example) Michael Jackson marrying Lisa Marie Presley. In local Pennsylvania history, it is important that John Potts, the son of a blacksmith and grocer turned ironmaster, married Ruth Savage, the daughter of three ironmasters.

Any history of adoption

Adoption can be formal- through the courts- or informal, such as when a person is fostered by friends or other persons and becomes part of that family. Certain foundling homes gave the same last name to all the babies, and these are traceable. In some cases, the person is adopted by a relative for now-unknown reasons. And always, we have families where the child came from a difficult start or was voluntarily surrendered by the birth parent for better care.

Other name change reasons

Names can change for many reasons. Immigrants who come in not speaking the language may find their name changed for pronunciation reasons, or to the name of the place they came from. Hitler's relatives in the United States are living under a changed name for obvious reasons. Large families have been known to take a double name appropriate to their culture and split it down the middle to aid in identifying individuals better. Some have members change their names almost at will, to include a different description, to simplify a name to separate themselves from a tragic event, or simply to hide an old identity from the law and political changes.

Religious preferences

Religion is a funny thing, not haha funny but serious funny. There are still deep divides over who should have gotten leadership of the Islamic movement in the 7th century, over foot washing and other small tasks, over which prophets you believe in, in how many gods, etc. If you can pin down which faith a person followed, or where they are buried if in a church yard, that can help you find other relatives. But recall that even if a person starts off in one faith, they may end up in another. One person in the records started non-mainstream Quaker, went Free Will Baptist as a teenager, with a different Quaker spouse, an Episcopal father, and a militantly Methodist daughter. Catholics, Amish, and Jews are classically strict about marrying within your faith, risking communication barriers in the future. This of course varies from family to family and time to time, but remains a serious question.

Literacy

Literacy is not a new concept. It is just in recent years in the Western World that we compel school attendance among a larger population. There is an example of a very intelligent businessman and lawyer in the 18th century who argued in court and built all kinds of structures and ran a big family, etc.- but could not write his name. Literacy comes in levels, from understanding the culture to being to write on your own to reading Chaucer in the original 14th century English or Greek. How literate was your family member?

Indentured servant or slave

Many people have moved around the world and so forth not always by their own choice. Indentured servants were in debt to the ship owners for their passage, and had to work for wealthier folks for a set time to pay the debt off. The most recent case the author has heard of was in the 1950s, coming from Europe and not able to afford to travel. They could be younger children of families unable to inherit much, adventurers, or running from the law. They could also have been caught by the law and shipped over to form the new population of the colonies, male and female. If this last is the case, see if you can find out what the crime was. It may not be that bad. You are here today. Slavery was a little different. They were probably not willingly present especially at first, and could inherit that legal status based on their parentage. The key here is that we can not change was occurred before. You can not make slavery not happen, any more than you can have prevented the Civil War to save lives. The critical element is to get the names and the stories written down and documented to save what information we do have about people who were classically treated as invisible. Did that relative have a house she was proud of, or did they garden? Why did they choose the last name they used at whatever point the decision could be made? Where did they worship? Were they literate? What work did they do? Were they emancipated by an owner, payment by a family member, or by the mass pronunciation of law?

Slaveholder

Yes, the flip side of the previous question. If your ancestor is on record as a slaveholder, that was their choice, not yours. The best thing you can do is to acknowledge the fact, and see if you can pin down who they had, and what happened to them. Depending on the situation, some remained socially attached in a way even after freedom. In their day, slaves were valuable property that could help when horses and cattle and some steam were the best motive power there was. Slavery has existed since living cultural memory. This is not to say that the arrangement would work well today in our culture, but again, try not to judge the past by today's standards.

Sources

There are many sources you can use to get more information, aided by the internet revolution. First steps should include making a checklist and talking to family, friends, and neighbors. Record what you learn and already are sure of in your immediate family. Local governments will have tax records and census records. Then try visiting the local historical society to use primary sources such as directories, cemetery notes, church records, old newspapers, family bibles, photographic collections, huge collections of obituaries, yearbooks, and the collected letters, documents, and items that may pertain. Secondary sources include books written by others about your interest area, hopefully properly cited as to the source of the information. Third, once you are sure of a clean start, consider a membership in an online service, such as ancestry.com. It can get more expensive than your local library, but is cheaper than travelling overseas for months to go through tax records. It can also be interactive with others who are researching the same family branches.

Keep a file with all your notes and information as well as a clean summary. Consider copying and sharing this information with your children and other family members to ensure the only copy is not lost to circumstances. Also, consider sharing a copy with your local library or historical society and/or publishing it officially to outside folks for research purposes. They can become valuable resources down the line, along with preserving the known artifacts from a family for future generations to ponder.

Summary

Genealogy is not an exact science. Always there remains some mystery around people, as they lived their own lives. And inevitably, there are the stories that were suppressed in the past and do come to light. Some families are touchy about anything from a change of faith or an illegitimate child to the reason for a death. The important information is still there, and should be recorded. History has already happened, and should not be judged for perfection, nor should it be ignored in the name of sanitation to modern standards. As the state- issued poster puts it, go ahead and shock Aunt Petunia!

Seriously, there are ways to tell a story about even a difficult subject without disrespecting those who participated. Cultural norms change even within a lifetime. One can not imagine, in the modern world, women not being allowed to have their own credit history or mortgage, as was legal not sixty years ago. Imagine the changes over the last hundred years, with electricity and changes in media and civil rights. Or over the last thousand years, with the Church/State balance shifting so radically, the medical breakthroughs, and all the political changes. Or over the last one hundred thousand years, when our ancestors were still recognizably related and living all over the world in their own ways, already sharing measurable DNA elements and eventually many common social practices including burial, marriage arrangements, trading for resources, and increasing speech patterns.

Working the trees backwards and sideways can increase your immediate sense of community, and of family you did not realize you had. Our ancestors survived plagues, foul weather, sea voyages, ice ages, droughts, walking over whole continents on foot, primitive medicine, etc., and we are all still here. How did we get here? What can we learn?

About the Author/Bibliography

The author is a historian, genealogist, and archivist for the local historical society and assists with research and living history for the local town founder's property. She has used family genealogies for her own and other trees for the information above, all of which can be found on the trees stored on ancestry.com and in digitized books, such as Mrs. James' Potts Memorial (originally published in the 1880s). In addition, try digitized newspapers such as newspapers.com for information about then-current events.

Please consider supporting your local libraries and archives by contributing your time, volunteering to assist with projects, combing the local stores for any pertinent items to be preserved, or donating to ongoing preservation efforts.